BEETHOVEN
PIANO SONATAS
VOLUME II
Nos. 16–32

Edited by Robert Taub

The commentary on the sonatas has been excerpted and abridged from
Playing the Beethoven Piano Sonatas by Robert Taub, published by Amadeus Press,
distributed by Hal Leonard Corporation.

On the cover:
The Wanderer above the Sea of Fog, 1818 (oil on canvas)
by Caspar David Friedrich
(1774–1840)
Hamburger Kunsthalle, Hamburg, Germany/The Bridgeman Art Library Nationality

ISBN 978-1-4234-0393-7

G. SCHIRMER, *Inc.*

DISTRIBUTED BY

HAL•LEONARD®
CORPORATION
7777 W. BLUEMOUND RD. P.O. BOX 13819 MILWAUKEE, WI 53213

www.schirmer.com
www.halleonard.com

CONTENTS

HISTORICAL NOTES

Ludwig van Beethoven (1770–1827)

THE PIANO SONATAS

In 1816, Beethoven wrote to his friend and admirer Carl Czerny: "You must forgive a composer who would rather hear his work just as he had written it, however beautifully you played it otherwise." Having lost patience with Czerny's excessive interpolations in the piano part of a performance of Beethoven's Quintet for Piano and Winds, Op. 16, Beethoven also addressed the envelope sarcastically to "Herr von Zerni, celebrated virtuoso." On all levels, Beethoven meant what he wrote.

As a composer who bridged the gulf between court and private patronage on one hand (the world of Bach, Handel, Haydn, and Mozart) and on the other hand earning a living based substantially on sales of printed works and/or public perform-ances (the world of Brahms), Beethoven was one of the first composers to become almost obsessively concerned with the accuracy of his published scores. He often bemoaned the seeming unending streams of mistakes. "Fehler—fehler!—Sie sind selbst ein einziger Fehler" ("Mistakes—mistakes!—You yourselves are a unique mistake") he wrote to the august publishing firm of Breitkopf und Härtel in 1811.

It is not surprising, therefore, that toward the end of his life Beethoven twice (1822 and again in 1825) begged his publishers C.F. Peters and Schott to bring out a comprehensive complete edition of his works over which Beethoven himself would have editorial control, and would thus be able to ensure accuracy in all dimensions—notes, pedaling and fingering, expressive notations (dynamics, slurs), and articulations, and even movement headings. This never happened.

Beethoven was also obsessive about his musical sketches that he kept with him throughout his mature life. Desk sketchbooks, pocket sketch-books: thousands of pages reveal his innermost compositional musings, his labored processes of creativity, the ideas that he abandoned, and the many others—often jumbled together—that he crafted through dint of extraordinary determi-nation, single-minded purpose, and the inspiration of genius into works that endure all exigencies of time and place. In the autograph scores that Beethoven then sent on to publishers, further layers of the creative processes abound. But even these scores might not be the final word in a particular work; there are instances in which Beethoven made textual changes, additions, or deletions by way of letters to publishers, corrections to proofs, and/or post-publication changes to first editions.

We can appreciate the unique qualities of the Beethoven piano sonatas on many different levels. Beethoven's own relationship with these works was fundamentally different from his relationship to his works of other genres. The early sonatas served as vehicles for the young Beethoven as both composer and pianist forging his path in Vienna, the musical capital of Europe at that time. Throughout his compositional lifetime, even when he no longer performed publicly as a pianist, Beethoven used his thirty-two piano sonatas as crucibles for all manner of musical ideas, many of which he later re-crafted—often in a distilled or more rarefied manner—in the sixteen string quartets and the nine symphonies.

The pianoforte was evolving at an enormous rate during the last years of the eighteenth century extending through the first several decades of the nineteenth. As a leading pianist and musical figure of his day, Beethoven was in the vanguard of this technological development. He was not content to confine his often explosive playing to the smaller sonorous capabilities of the instruments he had on hand; similarly, his compositions demanded more from the pianofortes of the day—greater depth of sonority, more subtle levels of keyboard finesse and control, and increased registral range. These sonatas themselves pushed forward further development and technical innovation from the piano manufacturers.

Motivating many of the sonatas are elements of extraordinary—even revolutionary—musical experimentation extending into domains of form, harmonic development, use of the instrument, and demands placed upon the performer, the piano, and the audience. However, the evolution of these works is not a simple straight line.

I believe that the usual chronological groupings of "early," "middle," and "late" are too superficial for Beethoven's piano sonatas. Since he composed more piano sonatas than substantial works of any other single genre (except songs) and the period of composition of the piano sonatas extends virtually throughout Beethoven's entire creative life, I prefer chronological groupings derived from more specific biographical and stylistic considerations. I delve into greater depth on this and other aspects of the sonatas in my book *Playing the Beethoven Piano Sonatas* (Amadeus Press).

1795–1800: Sonatas Op. 2 no. 1, Op. 2 no. 2, Op. 2 no. 3, Op. 7, Op. 10 no. 1, Op. 10 no. 2, Op. 10 no. 3, Op. 13, Op. 14 no. 1, Op. 14 no. 2, Op. 22, Op. 49 no. 1, Op. 49 no. 2

1800–1802: Sonatas Op. 26, Op. 27 no. 1, Op. 27 no. 2, Op. 28, Op. 31 no. 1, Op. 31 no. 2, Op. 31 no. 3

1804: Sonatas Op. 53, Op. 54, Op. 57

1809: Sonatas Op. 78, Op. 79, Op. 81a

1816–1822: Sonatas Op. 90, Op. 101, Op. 106, Op. 109, Op. 110, Op. 111

From 1804 (post-Heiligenstadt) forward, there were no more multiple sonata opus numbers; each work was assigned its own opus. Beethoven no longer played in public, and his relationship with the sonatas changed subtly.

—*Robert Taub*

PERFORMANCE NOTES

For the preparation of this edition, I have consulted autograph scores, first editions, and sketchbooks whenever possible. (Complete autograph scores of only twelve of the piano sonatas—plus the autograph of only the first movement of Sonata Op. 81a—have survived.) I have also read Beethoven's letters with particular attention to his many remarks concerning performances of his day and the lists of specific changes/corrections that he sent to publishers. We all know—as did Beethoven—that musical notation is imperfect, but it is the closest representation we have to the artistic ideal of a composer. We strive to represent that ideal as thoroughly and accurately as possible.

Tempo

My recordings of these sonatas are available as companions to the two published volumes. I have also included my suggestions for tempo (metronome markings) for each sonata, at the beginning of each movement.

Fingering

I have included Beethoven's own fingering suggestions. His fingerings—intended not only for himself (in earlier sonatas) but primarily for successive generations of pianists—often reveal intensely musical intentions in their shaping of musical contour and molding of the hands to create specific musical textures. I have added my own fingering suggestions, all of which are aimed at creating meaningful musical constructs. As a general guide, I believe in minimizing hand motions as much as possible, and therefore many of my fingering suggestions are based on the pianist's hands proceeding in a straight line as long as musically viable and physically practicable. I also believe that the pianist can develop senses of tactile feeling for specific musical patterns.

Pedaling

I have also included Beethoven's pedal markings in this edition. These indications are integral parts of the musical fabric. However, since most often no pedal indication is offered, whenever necessary one should use the right pedal—sparingly and subtly—to help achieve legato playing as well as to enhance sonorities.

Ornamentation

My suggestions regarding ornamental turns concern the notion of keeping the contour smooth while providing an expressive musical gesture with an increased sense of forward direction. The actual starting note of a turn depends on the specific context: if it is preceded by the same note (as in Sonata Op. 10 no. 2, second movement, m. 42), then I would suggest that the turn is four notes, starting on the upper neighbor: upper neighbor, main note, lower neighbor, main note.

Sonata in F Major, Op. 10 no. 2:
second movement, m. 42, r.h.

However, if the turn is preceded by another note (as in Sonata Op. 10 no. 2, first movement, m. 38), then the turn could be five notes in total, starting on the main note: main note, upper neighbor, main note, lower neighbor, main note.

Sonata in F Major, Op. 10 no. 2:
first movement, m. 38, r.h.

Whenever Beethoven included an afterbeat (Nachschlag) for a trill, I have included it as well. When he did not, I have not added any.

Footnotes

Footnotes within the musical score offer contextual explanations and alternatives based on earlier representations of the music (first editions, autograph scores) that Beethoven had seen and corrected. In areas where specific markings are visible only in the autograph score, I explain the reasons and context for my choices of musical representation. Other footnotes are intended to clarify ways of playing specific ornaments.

Notes on the Sonatas[1]

SONATA NO. 16 IN G MAJOR, OPUS 31 NO. 1 (1802)

Sonata Op. 31 no. 1 is a genuinely funny piece. Before starting it I try to put myself into the frame of mind of a pianist—perhaps a nervous pianist—who cannot seem to play chords together the right hand anticipates the left by a sixteenth note. This "problem" is brought to the musical forefront by Beethoven's gentle mocking humor.

This sonata is inherently a thoroughly well-crafted and even forward-looking work. Following the initial G-major statement of the main theme of the **Allegro vivace**, this theme is repeated immediately in m. 12 but in F major rather than in the expected dominant. The *forte* dynamic here is important; it is integral to the daring harmonic surprise, the first instance of this sort in the piano sonatas.

Although the development area is almost devoid of dynamic markings from the *forte* in m. 126 until the *forte* m. 170 (except for several *sforzandos*, mm. 140 and 148, and then mm. 158–161), the contour of the lines and changes of harmony imply the nature of dynamic shaping. With each new harmony—corresponding to the top of each new line—and the associated feelings of tension, I play more strongly. A new twist is added to the "problem" of the hands yet again at the end of the development: if the hands still can't play together in the normal position, they certainly cannot when the left crosses over the right.

Throughout this movement, dynamics, touch, and character of playing are crucial to conveying the humor. For example, playing the sixteenth-note difference between the two hands accurately, but in a way that seems to yearn for correction, and waiting the full measure rest before the last two chords, but playing them in an understated way, will convey both the frustration and humor of not being able to play with the hands together for virtually the entire movement.

Adagio grazioso is a good-natured parody of Italian lyric opera, in which the "diva" goes off or extraordinary runs and trills, leaving the "accompanist" wondering what to do. It thus becomes important to keep the three parts (two solo "singers" and "accompanist") separate and independent. Sometimes I allow the "singer" hand to take additional freedom of time, which means that the other hand must comply with flexibility in accompanying. In m. 26 when the trill under a fermata extends into a cadenza, I try to shape it as a vocalist might, both in dynamics and speed: starting the figure by allowing it to grow out of the trill, shaping upward to the high F and then gradually down away from it.

In the contrasting middle section, using pedal to connect the right hand would interfere with the staccato feeling of the left. If pedal is used at the beginning of each left-hand figure, it should then be lifted for the detached notes, and the right hand can be connected by judicious changing of fingers on the octaves.

The **Rondo: Allegretto** continues with long, flowing lyrical lines alternating between the two hands, which assume ridiculously funny extremes of tempo and dynamics in the coda. It is charming and graceful, demanding finesse, and is understated in its pianistic challenges. When the main theme is played in the bass (m. 16–17), the right-hand accompaniment can be soft, shaped, and flowing, with carefully articulated fingers held close to the keys and with a minimum of pedal. In the development, as minor-key versions of the theme are explored and a fugato established, the intensity of touch increases, and the theme is played *forte* for the first time. In the coda, elements of the theme are reconsidered in different tempos—Adagio alternating with tempo primo—and I use different qualities of touch for different contexts. The Adagio measures, for example, suggest a fuller sonority, not just because the second is marked *forte* (but the first is not), but also because of the slower tempo and fuller chords.

SONATA NO. 17 IN D MINOR, OPUS 31 NO. 2 ("Tempest") (1801–02)

Sonata Op. 31 no. 2, the "Tempest," is a brooding work, starting from the opening rolled chord in the **Largo/Allegro**. The first six measures—improvisatory and concentrated—are not merely introductory but rather form a strong motivic and spiritual foundation for the remainder of the movement, and in fact, the entire sonata. The opening should create harmonic suspense, for the

1 Excerpted from *Playing the Beethoven Piano Sonatas* by Robert Taub
edited and abridged by Susanne Sheston
© 2002 by Robert Taub
Published by Amadeus Press
Used by permission.

true harmonic setting of the first A major rolled chord is not yet defined. In m. 6, for the first time in the piece there is a sense of forward direction. With the left-hand six-four chord in m. 19 and the longest line in the right hand so far, a firm harmonic grounding begins to seem likely. I make the chromatic right hand smooth and the left-hand *sforzando* incisive, setting up the move to D minor in m. 21.

When we hear the largo measures after the exposition, we cannot know what follows. Three consecutive arpeggiations are a new idea, but the arpeggiations span a greater registral range here. Since they are not rolled chords, I play them slower and with more questioning feelings than the opening largo measures. The fermatas on the last note of each are held a long time, but the rests following the first two are strictly in tempo. Only the last note of this chain—the A-sharp—is held directly into the next measure with no break in sound. I tend to hold this last fermata the longest of the three, for the surprise explosive return of the main theme in F-sharp minor is the first *fortissimo* of the movement.

When the A major arpeggiation of the opening finally recurs, the prolongation of the expected home key is a pivotal factor in the extraordinary recitative that follows. Changing the pedal indication within this phrase (Beethoven's own), as unusual to us as the pedal marking might initially seem, destroys the line of the music.

The **Adagio** begins also with a rolled chord, but this time it is a stable, root-position chord. Accordingly, I play it with more of a definite feeling, rolled straight to the top, no hesitancy or coming away from the bottom note as in the initial rolled chord of the first movement. The division of the theme into two registers—as first encountered in the main theme of the Allegro—is reversed here, with the top line answered by the lower chords. The touch here is open, singing, and relaxed, opposite to that of the entire first movement. Recurring left-hand thirty-second-note triplets can help build intensity with touch and dynamics when the music suggests, such as in the crescendos beginning in m. 24 and in m. 39.

When the main theme recurs in m. 50, I try to make the left-hand embellished accompaniment as light and fluid as possible. The left hand plays over the right, with flat fingers and light pedaling. A particularly dramatic moment is the solo left-hand bass B-flat making a crescendo to the low A, *piano subito*, in mm. 91–92. The bare A should not be rushed; when allowed to resonate for a full measure it suggests a darker harmonic image, one that may possibly return to D minor. In the final measure, there is no fermata; the music ends quietly.

The **Allegretto** sonata-form last movement is obsessive in its use of the arpeggiated chord, but in a thoroughly composed rather than stylistically improvisatory manner. As suggested by the careful voicing of the left hand, I give a slight extra stress to the sustained offbeat A's. This helps destabilize the tonic somewhat. The right hand is gentle, and I think it's important to maintain a pulse of three eighth notes per bar, rather than allowing the music to lapse into a single beat per measure.

I pedal lightly in the last three measures of the movement so that the arpeggio gathers in sonority only gradually, allowing the last D—finally root position—to be the most final.

SONATA NO. 18 IN E-FLAT MAJOR, OPUS 31 NO. 3 (1801–02)

Sonata Op. 31 no. 3, the only four-movement work of this opus, is an ebullient piece. The first movement combines the good humor of Sonata Op. 31 no. 1 with the improvisatory qualities of Sonata Op. 31 no. 2. However, unlike its brethren, Op. 31 no. 3 lacks a true slow movement, for the middle two movements are a lively Scherzo and a songful Menuetto.

An unexpectedly delightful aspect of performing this sonata is the good-humored, quizzical, unsettled sensation created at the very beginning of the work: the music starts, the harmonies are ambiguous, and the music slows down and stops after a crescendo on an unstable second inversion chord—all this in only the first six measures. The striking opening chords of the **Allegro** and the ensuing ritard and fermata are not merely introductory: they include the primary motive and constitute the first theme, and they are developed as such. The mood of the second theme immediately contrasts with everything heard previously, for it is more fully harmonically grounded, and the music progresses without interruption by ritardandos or fermatas. Intentional ambiguity of harmony returns to herald the development area and the recapitulation. The tonic key of E-flat is studiously avoided throughout the development section and first part of the recapitulation until the return of the second theme (m. 170). Hence, the bass line in mm. 169–170—all in the lowest register of Beethoven's piano—is important in setting up this theme and in imbuing its arrival with a sense of finality. The final eight measures of the coda finally firmly establish E-flat major, but the *piano* dynamic of the ascending staccato sixths and *forte subito* for the last two chords still maintain the element of good-natured surprise which is so much a part of this movement.

Next in this sonata is not a slow movement, as might ordinarily be expected, but rather an exhilarating, joyful **Scherzo: Allegretto vivace**. It retains some of the playful and improvisatory elements of the first movement: lilting *sforzando* markings abound, and poco ritard indications on repeated notes before cadence points, (e.g., mm. 14–15) allow the music to hover before regaining momentum.

The slowest movement of Op. 31 no. 3 is not an adagio but rather the **Menuetto: Moderato e grazioso**. The minuet is a lyrical duet between the top line and bass. The longer singing lines contrast with openings of both previous movements, and although the tempo is not slow, it can seem spacious and luxuriant. Playful registral offbeat jumps in the Trio (mm. 16–18) recall similar qualities of the Scherzo but in a much slower tempo. A thread of connection between the Menuetto and the following Presto is set up by the chain of alternating E-flat–D–E-flat pitches of the coda; these become an integral part of the left-hand accompaniment as soon as the Presto begins.

The **Presto con fuoco** starts quietly, but there is no harmonic ambiguity here; E-flat major is definitively established from the start. Although fast, the pulse should still remain a quick six beats per bar rather than two dotted quarter notes; this gives more tensile strength to the line and allows for a greater sense of forward drive. Although there are two initial cadences in the home key in the coda, neither is definite enough. The music continues playfully back in tempo after the ritardando of the second cadence, straying slightly from E-flat major with a brief chromatic excursion within a linear crescendo before the final *fortissimo* cadence.

SONATA NO. 19 IN G MINOR, OPUS 49 NO. 1 (1798)

The two Sonatas Op. 49 are both small pieces with two movements; their very intimacy is their greatest challenge to the performer. Their brevity, the succinct qualities of their themes, their limited registral range and scale of dynamics—all are smaller in scope than those of any sonata that Beethoven had composed previously. Even so, they are impeccably crafted and demand pianistic control, particularly finesse in voicing and dynamics.

Sonata Op. 49 no. 1 is the more somber of the two. The pacing of the **Andante**, in G minor, is gentle and ambling; the sobriety of character can easily be weakened by playing too fast. At the very beginning of the piece, I make a distinct dynamic differentiation between the songful, plaintive melody and the accompanying chords, but nevertheless voice the left-hand legato chords slightly to the top. The sixteenth-note accompanying figures in the second theme are then softer, more in the background, which helps to enhance the contrast in texture and character between the first and second themes. The loudest sustained part of the short first movement is the *forte* opening of the development area with the trills in both hands, but this fades back to *piano* by the fourth measure, the cadence on E-flat major. Although no dynamic is indicated, I make a subtle crescendo in mm. 62–63. Tension builds in these measures as the right hand ascends chromatically, preparing—as we hear retrospectively—for the main theme to reenter as a surprise, *piano subito*, in m. 64. I take a bit of time at the beginning of the last eight-bar phrase—the coda—as B-natural is introduced (m. 103) to change from G minor to G major. Tempo primo is resumed almost right away, and the piece ends quietly, in tempo, without a ritard, leaving us hanging, waiting for the next movement.

The ensuing **Rondo: Allegro** is lively, but the pulse is six eighth notes to the beat, not in two, and the tempo is determined by the speed of the sixteenth notes, not the eighth notes. The opening theme is confined to the middle register, as is the first theme of the Andante, and the weighting implied by the slur over the B–G is a subtle way of showing the change in character from the minor interval B-flat–G of the first movement. The light character of the Rondo's opening becomes slightly more intense with the second theme, which is back in G minor and includes crescendos to *forte*. Clear portrayal of mood among the alternating themes in this Rondo is among the most important aspects of the piece, particularly since the themes are so concise. In the area of greatest profusion of dynamic indications (beginning in m. 135) the motivic unit of the main theme is tossed playfully back and forth between the two hands in different registers before the coda concludes with them safely back in the right hand and two *fortissimo* cadential chords.

SONATA NO. 20 IN G MAJOR, OPUS. 49 NO. 2 (1796)

Sonata Op. 49 no. 2 provides a challenging opportunity to consider one's understanding of Beethoven's early compositional and performing style, for there are no dynamic markings whatsoever in the first edition. Modern editions are based on this first edition since the autograph has been lost, and any dynamic markings are simply editorial. In performance, therefore, in order to judge appropriate dynamics, one applies one's own understanding of Beethoven's style of this era, of how he integrated the musical elements: tempo, character of themes, harmonic and metrical relations, nature of pianism.

I begin the opening of the **Allegro, ma non troppo** with feelings of confidence, aplomb, and a touch of bravura, *forte*. Rather than dropping to *piano* in m. 2 with the start of the slur (as is the case in some editions), I prefer to carry on in *forte* until the phrase winds down in m. 4, at which point I make a slight decrescendo, only to begin the repeat of the theme *forte* again. The quiet and more registrally confined second theme, which begins at the end of m. 20, can be *piano* until m. 36, which is again more brilliant. The development also begins *forte*, but then I drop immediately to *piano* for the triplet in the second half of m. 53. This change in dynamics contributes to feelings of surprise and anticipation, for the mode is minor for the first time and there is some question as to where the music is leading. Aside from the next *forte* motivic half note (m. 56)—which is now in A minor—I like to maintain the level of *piano* for the remainder of the development, but the arrival of the main theme back in G major is *forte*.

The second movement is marked **Tempo di Menuetto**. The theme is basically *piano*, and the two contrasting episodes are *piano* and *forte* respectively. The ways in which each episode leads back to areas of the main theme are simple, elegant, and balanced: the first via the right hand, and the second via the left.

The coda, beginning in mm. 107–108, introduces rests into the dotted figure of the main theme which, as the line descends, make it feel both more airy and more resigned. One could build drama with a crescendo as the line then ascends, but I think it is most in keeping with the intimate, impeccably crafted nature of this sonata to end the last chords softly, foregoing any temptation toward a more brilliant *forte* ending.

SONATA NO. 21 IN C MAJOR, OPUS 53 ("Waldstein") (1803–04)

The expressive qualities of Sonata Op. 53 pushed to new heights the limit of what could be demanded from the piano. Virtuosity is demonstrated not exclusively through loud playing but rather by exquisite control: each movement of the "Waldstein" Sonata begins *pianissimo*, and among the most frequently used dynamic markings is *sempre pianissimo*.

Op. 53 is the first of the post-Heiligenstadt sonatas, and, along with his Symphony No. 3 ("Eroica"), immediately and palpably demonstrates Beethoven's extraordinary resolve to continue to develop his artistry. Both the "Eroica" Symphony and the "Waldstein" Sonata are strikingly original— even revolutionary. In both, the sonata form is expanded well beyond its previous conceptions.

The importance of the role of the first note, the bass C, cannot be overemphasized. I weight the left-hand chords slightly to the bottom, preserving the low C's all the way throughout mm. 1–2 and continuing the vector-like chromatic descent to the G octave in m. 11. This descent helps infuse the work with its unique tension and urgency. The first right-hand chord comes in very softly, almost secondary to the low C. Although the harmonic motion is striking, it actually proceeds quite slowly; therefore, I like a fast tempo—**Allegro con brio**, *pianissimo*—creating the feeling that the opening chords are pulsating restlessly.

The crescendo in mm. 21–22 continues all the way through to the *piano subito* in m. 23, setting up the arrival of B major dramatically. The B major harmony here must have a palpable presence; it cannot be too soft—it is marked only *p*, not *pp* as in the opening of the piece. Heard retrospectively as the dominant to E major, it helps establish the smooth transition to the second theme which is in the mediant key (E major), an unusual key relationship. In no previous sonata had Beethoven characterized the themes so strongly; the unexpected choice of key for the choralelike second theme enhances the overall contrast.

The marking for the second theme, *dolce e molto legato*, implies voicing the chords to the top (as initially indicated by the upper-voice stems). Both hands are legato, and changing fingering on several keys after playing them is frequently the only way to achieve a smooth, connected sound.

I consider this sonata to be in two movements, with the **Introduzione: Adagio molto** as a true introduction to the **Rondo: Allegretto moderato**. Unlike the Andante that Beethoven had originally intended as a second movement for this sonata, the Introduzione does not stand on its own musically; rather it is meant to prepare us expressively and emotionally for the Rondo that follows.

The pedalings designated by Beethoven at the opening of the Rondo, the very particular use of crossed hands, the *pianissimo*, the expansive harmonic rhythm, and the slightly raised dampers all make for extraordinary music. Removing any of these elements undermines the entire concept, a delicate and evanescent edifice that contributes mightily to the expressive revolution embodied within this work.

This Rondo is among Beethoven's most sophisticated, with sonata-like development and modulations, and careful and thorough markings. The two explosive middle episodes are in minor keys closely allied with the C major tonic—A minor (the relative minor) and C minor (the enharmonic minor). The leisurely pace suggested by the indication Allegretto moderato is in contrast to the driving pace of the first movement and the sense of inevitable forward motion generated by the descending chromatic bass—although slow—of the Introduzione. The brilliance of the Prestissimo coda, replete with octave glissandos and luminescent trills, is unprecedented.

I allow the tempo of the Prestissimo coda to be dictated by the speed required by the octave glissandos (m. 465); the tempo therefore is necessarily very fast. The harmonic motion here is actually quite slow, and we have heard the theme many times by this point in the piece. A very fast tempo to conclude the work is brilliant and rousing.

SONATA NO. 22 IN F MAJOR, OPUS 54 (1804)
Op. 54 is one of the least frequently performed Beethoven sonatas, and I'm not sure why. It is a novel and adventurous work. The first of its two movements is surprisingly not in sonata form, but is instead a highly stylized minuet. The second, which lacks a contrasting theme, extends our concept of what constitutes a sonata with so thorough a development of the main theme and its motivic fragments that a feeling of return is evinced when the main theme recurs in the home key, even though we have never really parted from it motivically. Although the entire sonata is considerably more concise than its immediate neighbors, viewed from within and therefore considering the restraints that Beethoven placed upon himself regarding the basic musical material of Op. 54—the tiny musical cells from which it evolves, the work is one of unexpectedly thorough and subtle development.

The feeling at the beginning of the **In tempo d'un Menuetto** is relaxed. Each of the two times the main theme recurs it is increasingly more embellished and therefore a bit more intense. There is no smooth transition from the first to the second theme; rather the *forte* octaves of the second theme interrupt the tranquility of the menuet. The two ideas could not be more disjunct, and they should be played that way.

The **Allegretto** is monothematic, with contrasts in mood and feeling evoked by an enormously rich harmonic palette rather than by contrasting themes. I elongate the trill at the end of the exposition ever so slightly (second ending, m. 20) to help subtly distinguish the surprise and daring move to A major that follows. With each new harmony in m. 37 on, as the bass descends chromatically, I make sure to grow in intensity as the right hand ascends. I do not play the octaves in the bass beyond the low F (m. 40) that are indicated in parentheses in some editions, for Beethoven's piano at the time did not go below this note. However, I voice the top of the previous octaves to the top note so that the line gives the impression of continuing downward with the following E (m. 41), even though the lower octave note drops out. The main thematic ideas are frequently interchanged between the hands, and are voiced accordingly. The left hand is more prominent than the right in mm. 45–46 even though the only dynamic marking is *forte*, but the opposite is true in the following two measures, where the initial indication is *piano*. Generally, whichever hand has the moving line is the more prominent. I take the repeat of the entire second section, which allows us to revel once again in the extraordinary density of harmonic changes in this *moto perpetuo* movement.

The coda is faster than the body of the movement. Its syncopated *sforzandos* are important, for they infuse the final cadential harmonies with a sense of unsettled urgency which is never fully resolved even in the final measure; hence the fermata over the last eighth rest.

SONATA NO. 23 IN F MINOR, OPUS 57 ("Appassionata") (1804–05)

The spare texture of Sonata Op. 57—the hands are not one but two empty octaves apart—lends a unique sense of tension to the opening of the **Allegro assai**, which is relieved only briefly by the harmonies in m. 3 and m. 7. Although the dynamic is *pianissimo*, I keep the fingers firm and pedal very lightly, maintaining a taut and sparing texture throughout the opening figures, not allowing any harmonies to accrue until the very last note of each figure. The pulse within each measure is twelve rather than four, resulting in considerably more inner tension and drive—driving force here being steady, forward propulsion, not necessarily sheer speed.

The pulse of twelve eighth notes per measure should not be allowed to lapse in the cascading arpeggio figure in mm. 14–15 and in the syncopated chords of mm. 17 and 20. In fact, a twelve pulse heightens the effect of syncopation here, which in turn adds to the overall excitement. The repeated left-hand notes beginning in m. 24 also keep up the tension. If the piano I am using is well regulated, I use the same finger (3) for each note and allow the key to come up just barely past the point of aftertouch before playing the next note.

It is always a challenge to control the soft dynamic of the low repeated C (m. 134 on) which grows out of the D-flat–D-flat–D-flat–C motive and over which the main theme reenters in the home key of F minor. The low C's immediately become softer, leading to the *pianissimo* indication in m. 135; I use as light a touch as possible to make them very soft so that they do not interfere with or obscure the top line in any way. In the coda, following a single-line restatement of the main theme throughout the full registral range of Beethoven's piano (and virtually all of ours as well), the movement concludes in a shimmer, quieter than it began (*ppp*). A ritardando here would be superfluous, for the pace of the music slows down naturally in the bass as the note values increase over the last three measures.

The second movement, simply marked **Andante con moto**, is a theme with three variations. The low register of both hands, the *piano e dolce* marking, and the relative stillness of the line and conservative harmonic motion convey a sense of comfort and tranquility, feelings in complete contrast to those of the first movement. For the theme and the first variation, I voice the right-hand chords slightly to the top and play the bass as a voice equal to this line. As the variations progress with increasing density of notes, they ascend registrally and increase in dynamic range. What Beethoven does following the third variation is revolutionary: the theme is repeated, or rather begins to be repeated, unadorned. The movement ends with a *pianissimo* diminished seventh chord under a fermata (m. 96), leaving us hanging until the next chord, *fortissimo*, interrupts the softness and acts as a bridge to the last movement.

The **Allegro ma non troppo** sustains harmonic tension until it reaches its tonic (F minor) in m. 20. While the nature of the sixteenth notes of the main theme directs us forward, the bass also engenders a strong sense of resignation. In m. 96, I like to show the thematic entrances in each hand with a slight accentuation, which is then taken up by the *sforzandos* and the beginning of each group of chords.

The coda of Sonata Op. 57 is marked Presto, faster than the rest of the movement. The two groups of massive *fortissimo* chords in the first part of the coda are tension-provoking tonic–mediant chords. I make sure to play the A-flat chords in mm. 316–317 with as much weight as possible, emphasizing the surprise of their presence and the lack of harmonic stability they contribute.

By contrast, when a solid F minor is attained in m. 325, the dynamic is only *forte*. I would be careful to grade these dynamics, especially since they are all on the loud side of the spectrum, to reflect harmonic and dramatic positions. *Fortissimo* is reached again in m. 341, signaling the end, for finally nothing but F minor is heard from this point until the last measure. The main theme of this movement is a whirlwind here, and the final two chords are pedaled separately to punctuate the ending.

SONATA NO. 24 IN F-SHARP MAJOR, OPUS 78 (1809)

Sonata in F-sharp Major, Op. 78, one of Beethoven's favorites, offers subtle glimpses into the future; the concentration on small thematic motives is characteristic of the organic, meticulously composed works of the last period, works in which every nuance is an integral part of the whole. Distinctions between melody and accompaniment begin to dissolve in Op. 78 as thematic motives of equal importance are frequently juxtaposed as counterpoint. The very nature of its closely interrelated themes demands that each be as fully characterized and realized as possible, played so as to distinguish each theme individually but nonetheless to weave them all into a carefully constructed luminescent musical fabric.

The opening figure of the **Allegro ma non troppo** is abstracted throughout the exposition, both melodically and rhythmically. In the development, as the same rhythmic figure forms a counterpoint to the right-hand sixteenth notes, I shape the subtle dynamics of the right hand to mirror the contour of the phrase.

Among the most expressive markings of the first movement is Beethoven's *te-nu-te* (holding back) which he specified in m. 24 (and again in m. 83) for three left-hand chords. I play these three beats at an immediately slower tempo, with a sonorous left hand and articulated right hand so that the first and fourth sixteenth notes of each beat receive a little extra weight. This pattern, of course, is another manifestation of the opening rhythmic cell.

The same dotted rhythm also forms the basis for the first of the two themes of the **Allegro vivace**. However, the rhythmic values are doubled and the metrical position is changed so that the figure begins on the downbeat. The feeling is thus completely different, much more akin to the half-cadence figure first played in mm. 31–32 in the first movement.

Another musical motive in the movement is the grouping of sixteenth notes by twos. The barring of these groups by twos rather than by the more conventional four sixteenth notes—and this is very clear in the autograph score—is a direct indication that Beethoven had in mind detached two-note groups (even though playing four notes in a group is sometimes easier) and that he intended the feelings of breathlessness that this treatment engenders as the second note of each group is detached from the first of the following. The left-hand line therefore should really be as legato as possible, contrasting vividly with the right-hand groups above it and creating a situation of further contrast when the two-note groups alternate

between the hands (m. 2 on).

In keeping with the jocundity of this movement, I like to hold the fermatas in mm. 175, 176, and 177 a long time, allowing the surprise to build with each harmony. I then play the final six measures back in tempo, with the left hand as the main line. The rambunctious character of this coda comes in complete contrast to the quiet dignity of the opening Adagio cantabile of the sonata; even though this piece lasts less than eleven minutes, it creates a fully expressive universe.

SONATA NO. 25 IN G MAJOR, OPUS 79 (1809)

So crisp and vibrant is the beginning of Sonata Op. 79 that a good performance will lift the spirits of everyone in the audience, carrying them along on soaring lines that—although they may sometimes seem to double back on themselves—always move listeners forward with unflagging energy. Before actually starting the piece, I hear the first eight measures in my mind, setting the lively musical character and the quick tempo, imagining the sharp but playful *forte* staccato touch for the opening chords.

The first movement is **Presto alla tedesca**; the term *tedesca* alludes to a German folk dance in rapid triple meter, popular in the first decades of the nineteenth century. Not surprisingly, Beethoven's treatment is highly sophisticated. The *forte* indication at the beginning of m. 8 is both unexpected and important to the drama, for it pushes forward the momentum of the phrase at a point where one would ordinarily expect the tonic cadence to conclude the phrase. At the end of the second theme area (m. 46), there is another surprise *forte* at a cadence; we are once again propelled past the point that would ordinarily be the end of the phrase.

Throughout the development the dynamics are terraced; that is, they are either *forte* or *piano*. The pedal markings—indicated only in *dolce* and *piano* contexts in the development section—help set new harmonic areas into relief. For each marking I depress the pedal only slightly, which helps create a veil of sonority.

The *forte* that marks the beginning of the recapitulation (mm. 123–124) is indeed pedaled, and the foot is depressed to the floor. There is nothing delicate about these measures; they are high-spirited and buoyant. I wait very slightly before each of the *forte* appoggiaturas introduced in m. 184, giving as great a sense of lift and playfulness to each as possible. The actual ending of the movement—the last three measures—is unique; there are no other Beethoven sonata endings like it. There are no repeated chords, no *forte* pronouncements of the tonic. I try to play the ascending arpeggio gracefully and flowing to the top by pedaling only lightly and not allowing sonority to accumulate.

The beginning of the **Andante** is also unusual for Beethoven. The simple melody and the gentle bass, along with a 9/8 meter, create the feeling of a Venetian gondolier's song. The Andante's eighth notes determine the tempo. I allow the pace to expand very slightly at the apex of the crescendo and decrescendo throughout the first phrase. With the change of key into E-flat major in m. 10 and the longer treble lines and running sixteenth-note accompaniment in the bass, it is important not to rush. The *sforzando* in the transition back to G minor (m. 21) is poignant, as is the portato touch in the penultimate bar. The eighth rests in the last bar surround the final chords with silence and a ritard would be superfluous.

A feeling of openness is immediately reestablished by the **Vivace**, which is back in G major. During the first time through the first phrase, the right hand is primary, but in the repeat, I bring out the left-hand line a bit more. In m. 9, though, when the hands are in unison, they are equal in voicing. In m. 34, before the first recurrence of the main rondo theme, I take a little extra time and exert a bit of extra weight on the C-natural, for this helps establish the home key of G major. Here the theme is still quiet, even though the left hand is embellished with triplets which I play very evenly. In m. 72, the sixteenth notes of the accompaniment provide an undercurrent of motion, making this the most intense occurrence of the theme. Over the last five measures of the movement, the crescendo begun in m. 113 continues through the first beat of m. 116, then I wait before the *piano subito*. Once again, the movement concludes in tempo—playfully but softly—with no ritard.

SONATA NO. 26 IN E-FLAT MAJOR, OPUS 81A ("Das Lebewohl") (1809)

Beethoven dedicated Sonata Op. 81a ("Das Lebewohl", as he preferred) to his friend and patron, Archduke Rudolph. The sonata's three movements portray the leave-taking, the absence, and the return of the archduke during the Napoleonic invasion of Vienna in 1809. The only one of Beethoven's

sonatas to embody an extramusical program, the events it portrays are central to its interpretation.

The opening **Adagio** introduces the motive (over which Beethoven wrote *Le-be-wohl*) with a sense of intimacy, *piano* and *espressivo*. Although the first measure of the joyful Allegro is in a new, fast tempo, I hold the first chord of m. 18 just a little longer than the beat would ordinarily be, as implied by the tenuto indication above it. I also try to play the left-hand chromatic descent clearly, giving an added dimension of strength to the music. When eighth notes are played beginning in m. 21, the left hand becomes lighter, but the right hand continues its crescendo up to the top B-flat octave, before which I like to wait just a tiny fraction of a second, postponing the *sforzando* with an imperial gesture.

The "Lebewohl" motive is the melodic basis for most of the development area, as it is played in a wide range of different harmonic settings as if the music is searching for just the right path to continue. The leave-taking becomes understandably more prolonged with the motive's repetition in its barest form beginning in m. 223, but the tempo remains steady. I take a little extra time on the poignant high C appoggiaturas in mm. 248 and 250, the final questioning phrases of this movement before the final crescendo beginning with the octave C's (m. 252) ensures that the movement finishes strongly, in tempo.

The second movement—"**Abwesenheit**" (absence)— is not a slow, songful Adagio but rather a restless Andante espressivo. In mm. 13 and 14, as the musical line takes flight, I still maintain a pulse of four to the measure, increasing the weight of touch with the portato marking at the end of m. 14 and playing with a decidedly more singing tone as the legato line enters in m. 15. An altogether different quality of sound, one more mysterious and intense, is invoked by the subtle use of the right pedal in mm. 37 and 39. As with such markings earlier, I depress the pedal not fully to the floor but just enough to raise the dampers off the strings, allowing them to vibrate freely for the duration of the pedal marking.

I know of no greater outpouring of musical exuberance than the first ten bars of the third movement, "**Wiedersehen**" (return). These measures are extremely brilliant and virtuosic. Following the first chord, I drop in dynamic only to let it rise again as the line does. The diminuendo in m. 5 continues until the *forte subito* in m. 9, and once again, I drop to a lower dynamic level to start the rising line, which I play without slowing down, with increasing intensity in touch and dynamics.

Even the quieter second theme is brilliant in its extroversion. Crescendos and decrescendos are shaped by the inside measured trills beginning in m. 53. When the right hand plays off the beat (m. 69 on), I make sure not to pedal too heavily, so that the left hand remains clear and the main beats are not lost in a mass of too much sound.

The coda is marked *poco andante*, which I interpret to mean that each eighth note of the 6/8 meter is heard at a walking tempo. The pace really is quite a bit slower, considering that the body of the movement is at a most lively tempo. I like to consider the beginning of this coda as quasi-improvisatory, and I allow the pulse to be quite flexible. The final flourish leads to an emphatic cadence.

SONATA NO. 27 IN E MINOR, OPUS 90 (1814)

Before beginning to play Sonata Op. 90, I hear in my mind not only the notes and character of the first several measures—specifically the brusque, declamatory opening *forte* line G–G–F-sharp–E–A, complete with E minor harmony and rhythm—but also the *dolce* E major beginning of the second movement, a gesture of opening one's soul. One can hear the beginning of the first movement not only as the first phrase of the piece, but also as representing a defining element with which the entire second movement contrasts. After vividly imagining in my inner ear the feelings that the two first phrases conjure, I then rehear the opening of the first movement, setting the mood internally, and begin to play.

There is a quality of gruffness to the rhetorical opening of the **Mit Lebhaftigkeit und durchaus mit Empfindung und Ausdruck**. The answer to the question posed by these chords is *piano*, beginning with the last beat of m. 2. The interplay between gruffness and lyricism continues with lyricism winning out; the line begun with the last beat on m. 8 is the longest of the movement. I relish the beguiling way this line begins, particularly with the chromatic left hand (E–E-flat–D) in mm 10–11, and make it as smooth as possible.

Feelings of resignation are conjured by this movement. The large registral leap down from E to F-sharp (mm. 17–18) contributes to this within a crescendo; so do the fermatas (m. 16

and m. 24) at the end of first and second phrases. Scales that tumble down the keyboard beginning in m. 29 more than fill in the interval of the two previous registral leaps down, yet these scales are not sparkling; they are more into the keys, more introverted. When the B-flat of m. 39 changes enharmonically to A-sharp in the next bar, I like to voice the chord slightly to the top, allowing the mystery of the B-flat–A-sharp duality to continue as long as possible. In m. 82, the music is reduced to a slow pulse on a single repeated *pianissimo* B—which cannot be rushed—before the main theme returns, ascending and with increasing tension, in the development area.

There is a fermata over the last rest of the first movement, and I do not pull back from the keyboard when the music stops. Rather, I focus on preparing to begin the second movement without any interruption.

I begin the second movement **Nicht zu geschwind und sehr singbar vorgetragen** in tempo—avoiding a possible temptation to begin the first several notes slower, reaching the main tempo with the first full chord—simply because Beethoven marked *teneramente* (from *tenerezza*—tenderness) when the opening music returns in m. 24. The interpretive implication is to save the idea of beginning the phrase slower until the specific indication: doing something once is expressive; twice is a mannerism.

In m. 60 (and similar places) where the music seems to slow down as the bass changes from four sixteenth notes per beat to three triplets, keeping a steady and consistent pulse is important, avoiding the tendency to rush. Tension builds as the right hand ascends (beginning in m. 107) and the left descends, but grading the crescendo and eventual *forte* differently in each hand, with less strength in the bass, will allow the top to be heard all the way through, particularly the long D–F chord (mm. 110–111).

Shortly before the coda begins with the theme in the tenor range (m. 230), a melodic fragment of the theme is isolated and developed into a canon with a hint of chromaticism. This is the only area (beginning in m. 212) of real harmonic tension in the movement, and it is *pianissimo* throughout. Beethoven even wrote *sempre pianissimo* in the measures of enharmonic changes (mm. 216–218) to guard against an increase in dynamics. Tension is achieved by a penetrating quality of touch and by perhaps taking a little extra time.

SONATA NO. 28 IN A MAJOR, OPUS 101 (1816)

Although the first movement **Etwas lebhaft und mit der innigsten Empfindung: Allegretto, ma non troppo** of Sonata Op. 101 is quiet, with textures that are smooth and a tempo that is spacious enough for a pulse of six eighth notes per measure (not "in two"), feelings of unrest and even of yearning are engendered by avoidance of the tonic throughout. Intricate subtleties of voicing, dynamics, and phrasing are part of the master plan; not a stroke of the pen is wasted, nor is anything lacking.

The character of the second theme area is even more concentrated than that of the first theme, with Beethoven forging a new phrasing indication in m. 16—a double slur and a staccato mark—to reveal a new level of expression. I play each grouping as a single unit, with the most weight on the first note, which is connected as smoothly as possible to the second note, then a slight lifting of the finger before and after the third note. The dotted quarter note that follows, although obviously held longer, is not necessarily heavier; too much weight would spoil the delicately constructed questioning spirit of the group.

The *molto espressivo* indication (m. 52) for the series of carefully voiced chords before the false recapitulation (in A minor) implies a slight lessening of the tempo and a deepening of touch. I regain the primary tempo in m. 58.

The march-like feeling of the scherzo **Lebhaft. Marschmäßig: Vivace alla Marcia** derives from the ubiquitous sixteenth-note dotted rhythms. Often the feeling of lift is generated by sixteenth rests on the second half of the beat. Too fast a tempo— or an inaccurate pulse—can obscure all this and lead instead to a feeling of three divisions per beat (rather than four) if the final sixteenth note of each beat is too slow relative to the quarter-note pulse. Therefore in addition to the quarter-note pulse, I try to feel a very quick pulse of four within each beat to ensure that the sixteenth notes are not elongated into triplet eighth notes. An element of whimsy is introduced by the long pedal marking beginning in m. 30, gently blending together harmonies, *piano*, very unmartial, over a low D-flat pedal tone. I use a delicate touch here, taking a bit more time but still maintaining the impetus of the dotted rhythms.

The mood of the concise **Langsam und sehnsuchtvoll: Adagio, ma non troppo, con affetto** is established by the feeling of the first chord—Mit einer Saite; sul una corda (therefore with the left pedal depressed, *pianissimo*)—as a stark contrast to the exuberance of the second movement. To help preserve the arch of the sixteenth- and thirty-second-note figures, I avoid an accent on the third sixteenth of the beat. Also, I play all the grace notes beginning in m. 12 before the beat.

The character of the finale **Geschwind, doch nicht zu sehr, und Entscholssenheit: Allegro** is triumphant; tonal restlessness and searching have given way to unambiguous harmonic confidence and strength. Beethoven was concerned in varying degrees with fugue in each of his late piano sonatas, beginning with Op. 101, and the entire development section of the final movement is a four-part fugue in the enharmonic minor. The climax of the fugal development section is a statement of the entire subject in the bass. Beethoven made dramatic use of the low E almost three octaves below middle C here (available on his piano by 1816), and to ensure that no one would reproach him for erring (many pianos still extended only to the low F), Beethoven wrote *contra E* in the score. This low E ushers in the return to A major for the recapitulation, for the E is the starting point of a dominant arpeggiation spanning virtually the entire keyboard. From its quiet, lyrical, searching beginnings, Sonata Op. 101 draws to an exultant close.

SONATA NO. 29 IN B-FLAT MAJOR, OPUS 106 ("Hammerklavier") (1817–18)

Sonata Op. 106 is the longest of the Beethoven sonatas, infrequently played because of its extreme interpretive and pianistic challenges. Having lived with the "Hammerklavier" for eight years before performing it publicly for the first time, learning and relearning, experimenting, and then playing it in many concerts and recording it, I have come to relish its challenges, and realize that to play it well, concentration of total immersion is required.

In the **Allegro**, dramatic tension is engendered by a fundamental clash between the tonalities of B-flat major and B major (and B minor). The very opening of this movement is undeniably treacherous; particularly at tempo, it is easily possible to miss one of the notes of the chord. I make sure both hands are in position before beginning, and then look at the area of the keyboard of the first left-hand chord. Wherever the eyes are, the hand is sure to follow.

Every principal theme is closely related to this opening one, which is motivated by the interval of a third in both rising and descending gestures. (Every one of the five movements of this sonata is constructed with large-scale trajectories of descending thirds, as well as with themes whose principal motivating characteristic is the interval of the third.) The fermata over the quarter rest in m. 4 allows the reverberations of the enormous opening to dissipate and gives the performer time to prepare for the *piano* dynamic and legato touch of the melodic line that fills in the opening thirds. In m. 15, I make sure that the left-hand dynamic, even within the crescendo, does not overpower the intrepid right hand as it reaches to the top of the keyboard.

The development of the opening thematic motive is thorough and consuming. I make sure to begin the fugue quietly (m. 137) and in a very steady rhythm, a strict pulse of four beats per bar. This feeling exemplifies a sense of "working out" of the motive. In m. 201, the touch is again very different. I play the beginning of the B major area with very curved, intense fingers (as opposed to the flatter fingers in the previous four measures) to produce direct but thinner qualities of sound.

An infamous textual controversy in the Allegro concerns the area of the transition to the recapitulation (mm. 224-226). Within the key signature of B Major (five sharps), Beethoven did not mark a natural sign in front of each A (eight of them), and yet there is an argument that he meant to, but just forgot. An Artaria first edition in the Scheide collection has only the A (sharps), no natural signs. In the letters to Ries of the 20 March and 16 April 1819—those in which Beethoven detailed more than one hundred other corrections—he made no mention of this passage. Consistent with the nature of the movement and the expressive function of this transistion, the tritone of A-sharp-E generates far more tension than the bare fourth of A-E. Furthermore and perhaps most convincing, the recapitulation begins with a B-flat octave, not just a low B-flat note as in every other statement of this motive—the tenor B-flat is an enharmonic reinterpretation of the A-sharp that preceded it. The octave B-flat is also the reason that it is necessary to have a triple D in the left hand in m. 229; for the music's trajectory to continue, the third of the triad (rather than the root) is stressed. For all these reasons, I play A-sharps here.

In the recapitulation, the secondary theme is in G-flat major rather than in G major as it is in the exposition. The trill beginning in m. 338 is the only trill I know of in the entire literature that is surrounded by octaves in the same hand; I use the only fingering possible—2-3—except for m. 340, in which I use 1-2. Regardless of the quick tempo, it is important to allow the stark contrasts between *forte* and *piano* in the coda to be felt, as the G-flat—F-sharp tension resurfaces. Similarly, the pedal markings in the last five measures are very specific and help establish a rhythmic trajectory which, along with the progression of F–D–B-flat as the uppermost notes heard in the penultimate two bars, concludes the movement powerfully in B-flat major.

The **Scherzo: Assai vivace** second movement is much smaller in formal scope than the first movement. Repeating the top notes of each hand in the upbeat and downbeat figures is a challenge at the intended tempo. A piano adjusted for a large degree of aftertouch can be more responsive. Even so, I play the upbeats lightly, barely depressing the keys, so that the downbeat can be played with slightly more force. I begin the Presto area with a quarter-note pulse that is slightly faster than that of the previous music. Although the touch is light, the tempo cannot be too much faster if the offbeat right-hand chords beginning in m. 89 are to be clear. In mm. 106–112, I drop in dynamics for the prestissimo ascending run, which is light and gives the effect of being simply tossed off.

The **Adagio sostenuto** is among the longest and most dramatic slow movements that Beethoven composed in any genre. I keep an inner pulse of six beats per bar to avoid playing in a slow duple pulse. When the main theme begins to recur in m. 27, the left pedal is lifted as indicated by *tutte le corde*. I change the right pedal with every sixteenth note to avoid pedaling through the left-hand rests and negating their expressive qualities. As the surface motion slows considerably in m. 57, I make sure to maintain an even pulse to guard against rushing, allowing the harmonies their full due. In the area following the greatest emotional intensity, beginning in m. 107, Beethoven's expressive terms imply spaciousness of expression. Large registral spans in m. 118 and m. 121 also broaden the music physically (for the player) and aurally as well.

In no other Beethoven piano work are there more *una corda* and *tre corde* markings. These directives for the use of the left pedal relate not only to quantity of sound (soft vs. loud) but perhaps more importantly to quality of sound. A pianissimo sound can be more present if the strings are struck normally (*tre corde*) by the hammers, or it can seem more distant if the left pedal is depressed (*una corda*). Hence, the placement of *una corda* in m. 61 (and m. 145) has more to do with subtle timbral differences that come into play when the left pedal is depressed than with quantity of sound, since the dynamic is already very soft. The connection between the decreasing dynamics of the final two chords and Beethoven's *tre corde* indication—which may initially seem contradictory—is critically focused upon timbre.

I do not wait any longer than the silence of the last eighth rest of the Adagio before beginning the **Largo**. This movement is an improvisatory link between the Adagio and the Allegro risoluto. I begin each new theme somewhat tentatively, as if seeking the right path, but with the arrival of the third theme (G-sharp minor, m. 3) and its establishment of a more definite meter, we can feel as though we have finally found our way.

Although the chain of trills that begins the **Allegro risoluto** seems improvisatory, it is not and should not be played that way. The trills lead, with a direct and strong bass underpinning, to the theme which forms the basis for the entire fugal last movement. Although the entire movement has only one ritardando indication, I do allow the music to breathe, taking time to resolve cadences.

There is not much time for long trills in the intense stretto of mm. 233–236. In fact, just a short trill of three or five notes is sufficient; the main idea is a concentration on the leaps of a tenth, and the trill is simply a thematic reminder. The choralelike variation that follows is wholly unexpected and is played with a solemn and steady grace. Following the poco adagio, which serves notice that the end is near, *pianissimo* thematic fragments—played clearly and back in tempo—lead to the opening motive back in octaves in both hands. So interwoven is the emphasis on thirds that even the coda avoids a V–I cadence until the very end. Of course, I play these chords *fortissimo*, but I elongate the eighth rest before the penultimate chord by just a fraction of a second, giving the final cadence a little more drama and weight.

It is no secret that Beethoven became convinced of the necessity of metronome markings during the last decade of his life. The "Hammerklavier" is the only Sonata for which he ascribed metronome markings; that such markings should remain largely unrespected today is puzzling. It has been shown that Beethoven's metronome was not faulty, and that he took seriously the setting of tempi. It must be assumed that his metronome markings accurately reflect his hearing of the piece in his inner ear. Although pianists to this day have considered the metronome markings of this piece to be unplayable - too fast - except for the Largo, I disagree. Since Beethoven worked on Op. 106 for almost two full years and was fully immersed in its musical universe, for him the tempos were not unduly fast. True, they stretch the limits of pianism, but the work stretches the limits of musical perceptions on many levels.

SONATA NO. 30 IN E MAJOR, OPUS 109 (1820)

Sonata Op. 109 forges ahead in new ways, with new formal flexibility. The first movement is highly concentrated and compressed, the second—rather than being a slow movement—is extremely fast, and a theme-and-variation movement concludes the work.

The gentle opening of the **Vivace** arises from silence; there are no chords at the beginning, but harmonies accrue as the first note of each group is held through the beat. Rather than starting slightly under tempo and then reaching stride after the first measure or so, I prefer to begin softly and sweetly, but in tempo.

I make the sound of the first of the two notes in each right-hand group slightly heavier than the second, as implied by the quarter-note voicing, but both are sustained throughout the beat. The left-hand groups of two equally voiced sixteenth notes have an implied diminuendo within each group; the second of the two notes is slightly lighter than the first.

I make sure that I hold the pedal until the last sixteenth note in mm. 12–13 as the music of the beginning of the second theme is abstracted into a greater registral span, one that encompassed the full keyboard of Beethoven's instrument. With the *espressivo* marking at the beginning of m. 14, I expand in time as the music climbs ever higher, resuming the normal tempo for this area as the triplets begin to cascade downward.

A crescendo beginning in m. 42 leads to the registrally expansive recapitulation; the beguilingly simple character of the opening theme is now declamatory. When the second theme is repeated (including a *fortissimo* surprise move to C major), it ends in the home key of E major.

In the coda, I make sure the rests in mm. 75–77 are given full value. They are the only silences so far in this movement, and while the harmonies they offset are three pivotal harmonies in the movement, they also create feelings of suspense.

The **Prestissimo** second movement breaks in, *fortissimo*, without a silent pause, before the final chord of the first movement has completely died away. The pulse should be six per bar to avoid playing in two, but the tempo is very fast. To achieve this sort of speed, clarity is necessary. I use well-rounded fingers and only light pedaling. The touch, except when indicated legato by a slur, is lightly detached.

Ironically, the development area of this movement is quiet, although tension simmers beneath the surface. The main line here (m. 70 on) is formed from the bass at the opening of the movement. While the right-hand lines form a canon, intensity is maintained by articulating each note of the left-hand tremolandos. Use light pedal only, and keep a strict pulse of six. The crescendo in mm. 156–157 is challenging, particularly since there is an inclination to rush, but if the pulse is maintained, feelings of surging forward will be more suitably expressed.

In the **Gesangvoll, mit innigster Empfindung: Andante molto cantabile ed espressivo**, each eight-bar phrase of the theme is repeated, and each time I make sure the left hand is legato in the first three two-part units. As the theme becomes more abstracted in the second variation and the surface pacing increases, clarity of texture is paramount. I use either very light pedal the first time through, or none at all for the interlocking sixteenth-note areas. The third variation, Allegro vivace, is the most brilliant variation of the work. I make the detached eighth notes quite short here. This quick variation leads without pause into the next one, which is specified as being slightly slower than the theme. With the continuous addition of voices, I show the beginning of each with a slight increase of weight of touch. The fifth variation is a fugato; it is here that Beethoven abandoned use of the term "variation" since the form is not followed strictly. I make all the eighth-notes staccato and voice the lines as in a Bach fugue.

The final variation is the longest. In m. 5, I keep the pulse of the dotted quarter-note equal to that of the quarter-note in m. 4. As the epic trills of the movement begin, the melodic line and the harmonies of the theme are abstracted around trills first in the bass (not so loud as to obscure the top line) and then in the treble. In mm. 25-32 I use the fingering 1-2 for the trill and the fifth finger for the thematic line. Using the pedal as Beethoven suggested in m. 32 creates a *pianissimo* tonic-dominant mist out of which condenses a restatement of the theme, a simple stroke unprecedented in the sonata literature.

A question that inevitably arises for performances of any theme and variations concerns the seams between variations. Should time be taken? If so, how much? Should endings of final phrases be rounded off by slowing down, or remain in tempo?

A subtle hint in the autograph score, one that cannot be gleaned from any printed edition, addresses the issues for Sonata Op. 109. At the end of the theme, Beethoven had initially written *ritardando*. One would assume that this indication applies to the repeated statement of the end of the theme, thus adding to the closure of the theme and separating it somewhat from the first variation. However, after completing the autograph in ink, Beethoven crossed out this *ritardando* in pencil. He then added a *ritardando* and a low E in the bass (also in pencil) in the equivalent place when the theme is restated after the last variation, in the very last measure of the movement.

Since printed scores include no marking here whatsoever, an interpreter might consider a *ritardando* to be in good musical taste at this point. But Beethoven's explicit crossing-out of the *ritardando* at the end of the theme exerts an influence far beyond its immediate locus, as does the addition of the *ritardando* in the final measure of the movement. The interpretive implication of the deletion is that the theme flows seamlessly into the first variation, and the first into the second, and so on. I would not take time between any two variations, nor slow the ending of any until the final measure of the movement, since Beethoven was very explicit about the use of the term *ritardando* and about manipulating the perception of time. The journey through this movement is continuous—and the overall effect of the movement is cumulative—as the music becomes ever more abstract. When the end of the piece is finally attained, the singular *ritardando* in the last measure, the addition of the low E, and a pedal marking with no notated release for the last chord all frame the work in its own essence.

SONATA NO. 31 IN A-FLAT MAJOR, OPUS 110 (1821)

As I begin to play Op. 110, I am careful not to treat the first four measures of the **Moderato cantabile molto espressivo** as an introduction. They are in the moderato tempo—a stately three beats per measure—of the movement, not slower, and I voice the first two measures only slightly to the top. With the *piano subito* and fermata in m. 4, the pulse is flexible. I begin the D-flat trill (m. 4) with a pace that grows out of the sixteenth note that preceded it, increase the speed of the trill with the crescendo, and decrease it only slightly with the decrescendo for a smooth transition to the thirty-second notes that follow.

As the freer cadence in m. 4 leads to an intensely lyrical line over a gentle accompaniment (beginning in m. 5), the qualities of touch change with the right hand really singing out and the left becoming considerably quieter. The area around m. 12 demands an even, light touch, with very slight accentuations on the right-hand notes that Beethoven marked staccato. I make sure not to rush here, and I change the pedal frequently.

The concise development concentrates solely on modulating the harmonic context of the opening motive. Here, for the first time, harmonic motion is intensified, and the opening motive assumes subtly different shadings of mood. Beethoven's legato and dynamic markings are specific for each hand. With the emergence of the theme in a new key (D-flat major) but within the same registral area as m. 5, Beethoven added simply *dolce*. I drop down in dynamic level and play with a very lyrical tone, but maintain the tempo. The place to expand the pulse slightly is at the end of m. 66, as the D-flat prepares to be transformed enharmonically to C-sharp in m. 67.

The scalar second theme is in a lower register of the piano when it recurs in the recapitulation. In the coda, don't rush the first chord of each two-note group, but rather allow it to melt into the resolution. The last two chords of the movement are strictly in tempo, as are the quarter rests at the end of m. 116, and lead without pause into the Allegro molto.

Although the first movement concludes with rests, the pace continues uninterruptedly, with the first chord of the **Allegro molto** coming where the downbeat of the next measure would ordinarily be. Among the more immediate pianistic challenges of the Allegro molto is that of producing sharp, staccato chords with the right hand in m. 6 while maintaining a legato line with the left-hand octaves. Using pedal would lessen the staccato qualities in the right hand. The tempo is quick (but with a quarter-note pulse, not a half-note pulse) so that the change of fingering on the E octave has to be fast indeed. The two measures of rest (mm. 37–38) provide important drama and cannot be rushed. In the boisterous trio that follows, I use Beethoven's suggested fingering in m. 71.

Although the first three measures of the **Adagio ma non troppo** are of a single tempo, the music becomes highly improvisatory in m.4. Over the next four measures, there are six indicated changes of pacing. The long, unending songful melody begun in m.9 is among the most plaintive, beautifully lyrical lines in the literature. In the spirit of Arioso dolente and Klagender Gesang, the singing right hand floats above the left, although clear articulation of the subtle changes and the left hand's metrical insistence are integral to its mournful nature.

I begin the fugue subject that follows in an almost improvisatory manner. Although the tempo is strict, the sound quality is soft and gentle, as if the theme is being coaxed from the piano. I maintain a pulse of six beats per bar and keep the tempo (Allegro ma non troppo) steady throughout. The bass entrance of the theme in m. 73 three beats early is a jarring surprise, particularly with the *fortissimo*, but I do drop slightly in dynamic level in order to rise again as the ascent of the interval of the fourth continues into m. 80.

Among the most moving features of the second arioso is the way that the line breaks off in mid-phrase—as if quite literally breathing (or sobbing) quietly but passionately—the musical result of thirty-second-rests Beethoven introduced within the line (beginning in m. 120).

In the midst of the return of the inverted fugal subject, Beethoven places a double augmentation of the subject in counterpoint against a triple diminution: beginning in m. 152 the music is simultaneously twice as slow (top of the right hand) and three times as fast (left hand and inside of the right hand). When the fugue subject returns in tempo (m. 174, fourth beat), the texture is no longer strictly contrapuntal. I maintain the same tempo. The dynamic level is only *forte; fortissimo* is reserved for the final cadence. When the fugue subject becomes purely melodic (sforzando, m. 188) in this powerful ending of Sonata Op. 110

the affirmation—the journey of motivic, thematic, and emotional transmogrification—is complete.

SONATA NO. 32 IN C MINOR, OPUS 111 (1822)

Sonata Op. 111 is an enormous expressive challenge to pianists, to pianos, and to listeners, for no matter how many times we have played or heard this work, there are new aural connections to be made, deeper realms of emotional involvement, new perceptions to be felt.

The drama is riveting from the start. I sit up straight, and when I have heard the tempo of the opening measures internally and established the maestoso feeling of the opening to the **Maestoso**, I place my left hand on the first E-flat octave. I then look at the second octave that the left hand plays—the F-sharp octave—hearing once again the tension inherent in this diminished seventh interval, and only then do I play the first two chords, using the thumb as a guide to make sure that there are no extraneous notes. While the F-sharp octave is reverberating I place my right hand on its first chord and complete the first two-measure phrase, insuring that the trill receives special dynamic emphasis and that the chords in m. 2 are voiced subtly to the top, establishing a line beginning with B–C–D.

The first true theme, appearing in mm. 20–22, climbs registrally and in intensity; I find that Beethoven's suggested fingering is very helpful in this tricky passage. In m. 48, the right hand effectively unites the registers of the first theme. This confluence of register prepares for the second theme, which is an astounding contrast with the first. Its pace is flexible. I play this music with as sweet and gentle a touch as possible, but tension is still inherent in this theme. I play the elements of the first theme that return in m. 58 in a triumphant manner; finally the bass plays A-flat, and the harmony is stable.

As the key of D-flat is temporarily established in mm. 98–99, the impact of C minor is temporarily lessened, and I allow the pace to slow a bit with the *espressivo* and *poco ritenente* of m. 99. The recapitulation takes the theme to extreme registers of the piano, creating the effect of barely controlled drama.

I play the diminished chords in mm. 146–147 as strongly and emphatically as possible, changing touch with the first one in m. 148. Since the

chords are all off the main beats, the rests—held for their full duration, not rushed—are crucial for maintaining the metrical frame of reference here, and thus the backbone of the music. At the end of the movement, the final chord sounds hollow, for only the upper and lower registers are played.

From the start, the **Arietta: Adagio molto semplice e cantabile** evokes feelings of spaciousness. At the beginning, I play the left hand very quietly but make sure that the general sonority is full and round. The right hand is also quiet, although it is voiced to the top to bring out the arietta line. The point at which the line opens up the most is the apex of the crescendo in m. 6, after which the intensity diminishes. I change the quality of the sound markedly for the second part of the arietta, which begins in A minor.

In this movement, Beethoven integrated variation and sonata-allegro form, and the third variation is dramatically different from the first two. Beginning *forte*, the surface motion is twice as fast again as that of its predecessor. I drop in dynamics in the right hand as the left-hand arpeggios sweep up the keyboard. Following the third variation, the musical line becomes far more abstract, but the basic harmonic and metrical backbone is unchanged. I use the left pedal throughout the *pianissimo* area and change the right pedal with every right-hand rest.

Beethoven brings back the idea of the theme with a simple reaffirmation of the three basic harmonies (C major, A minor, G major; mm. 100-105). I play these measures as two groups of three, with a substantial crescendo in each. That of the second group goes all the way to the end of the phrase. We are then faced with the issue of how to continue.

The fundamental approach of classical variation diminution has brought the music to this point but can take it no further. So after restating the three fundamental harmonies, Beethoven brought in the ultimate in diminution (or speed) -the trill. The C-G-G motive is played, now *forte*, in the bass only, under the D-E trill. The trill also allows the music to dissolve, and the motive recurs in new, foreign harmonies as the trill changes to D-E-flat. At this point the music is no longer a further variation but is rather a nascent development of the generalized C-G-G motive in new harmonic contexts. The trills grow with the crescendo starting in m.114, and the bass B-flat in m.116 can be played truly sforzando, for the right-hand trill continues above it.

Development of the main thematic motive continues more explicitly in the measures that follow (mm.120-130). From m. 125 on, I keep the top line of the right hand as the main thread, while the left hand plays the light, subtle rhythmic outlines of the abstracted theme as begun in m. 120.

I elongate the last dotted eighth-note of m. 130, the only concession to the start of the recapitulation, and I keep the same tempo with which the movement began. Intensity reaches a peak in mm. 159-160, as all that is left is a trill on high G. As a near-final transformation, the theme is played with the trill in counterpoint, first above, then below. The left hand is a mere shimmer, the trills very soft, and the melodic notes not so much played as caressed.

Finally the motive C-G-G is itself inverted; it becomes G-C-C to end the sonata. This is a moment of transcendence; after nearly thirty minutes of music, time seems to stand still, even to reverse itself.

Final Thoughts

Beethoven's sonatas—as individual works, or taken together as a complete cycle—are pieces that we can listen to, learn, play, put away, relearn, and perform again over and over—with only increasing joy, involvement, and meaning. For those of you looking at the musical score as you follow a recording, welcome. For those playing these pieces for the first time, I invite you to become involved. And for those returning to these sonatas after learning them previously—or comparing this edition to any other—I invite you to roll up your sleeves and start playing, for there is always more to do. The expressive universe conjured up by the Beethoven piano sonatas is unprecedented, and unequalled.

—Robert Taub, editor

References

For sources consulted in researching this edition, please see the Bibliography in *Playing the Beethoven Piano Sonatas*, by Robert Taub, published by Amadeus Press (Hal Leonard Corporation).

Sonata in G Major

Opus 31 no. 1
Composed in 1802

Allegro vivace (♩ = 138)

16.

a) The fingering in italics is Beethoven's.

b) without tail

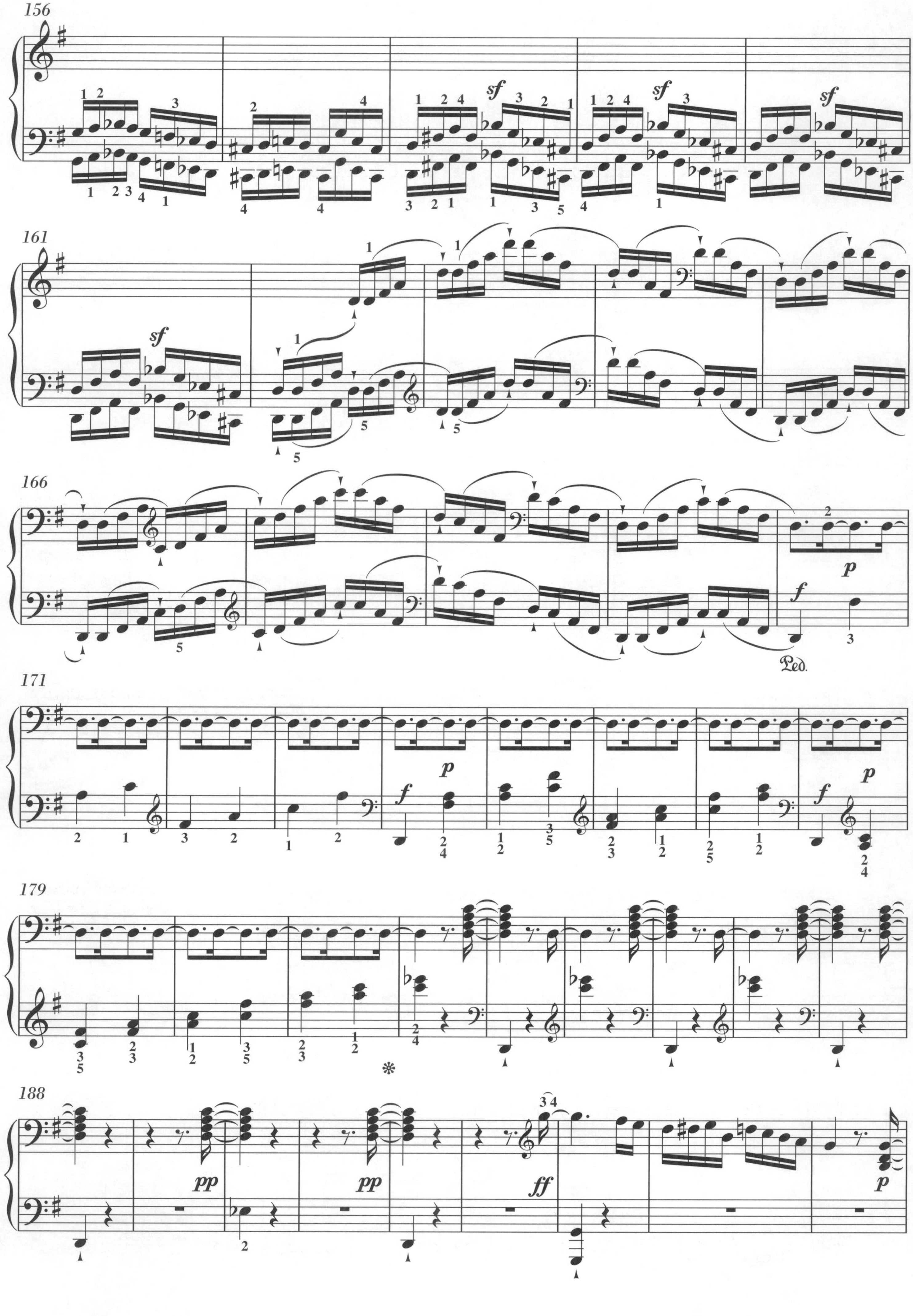
156
sf
161
166
p
f
Ped.
171
179
188
pp
ff

Adagio grazioso (♪ = 112)

c) G–B–D–F in the first edition (Cappi, Simrock)

d) The trills in mm. 99 and 100 are without tail.

e) Although all editions agree on the placement of the *sf* under the A-flat in m. 113, several early editions place the *sf* under the G in mm. 111 and 112. This lessens
the harmonic impact of the A-flat.

RONDO
Allegretto (♩ = 88)

f) B is the first eighth note as per the first edition. The G printed in some editions is incorrect.

Sonata in D minor

Opus 31 no. 2
Composed in 1801–02

17.

a) The fingering in italics and the pedal markings are Beethoven's.

30

b) l.h. over r.h.

c) Pedal off on fourth beat (with the 𝄽); same for m. 96

d) The D-flat on the final sixteenth-note in the first edition is a printer's error. In a copy owned by the Gesellschaft der Musikfreunde, it has been corrected by Beethoven to C.

36

38

g) with tail   h) with tail

Sonata in E-flat Major

Opus 31 no. 3
Composed in 1801–02

a) without tail

SCHERZO

Allegretto vivace [♩ = 104]

b) The F in this figure was the highest key on Beethoven's piano at this time, so the G and A-flat of the previous measure could not be played in this higher register.

60

64

MENUETTO
Moderato e grazioso [♩ = 76]

c) without tail

Presto con fuoco [♩. = 96]

d) without tail

72

Sonata in G minor

Opus 49 no. 1
Composed in 1798

19.

RONDO
Allegro (♩. = 92)

78

80

Sonata in G Major

Opus 49 no. 2
Composed in 1796

Allegro, ma non troppo (♩ = 76)

a) There are no dynamic markings included in the first edition (Kunst und Industrie-Comptoir, Vienna, 1805). All dynamic markings in this edition are suggestions of the current editor.

c) without tail

Tempo di Menuetto ($\quarternote = 100$)

Dedicated to Prince von Waldstein

Sonata in C Major

Opus 53
Composed in 1803–04

a) The fingering in italics, and the pedal markings are Beethoven's.

b) An early proof of the first edition erroneously printed an F-flat here. In the first edition, one can observe the "ghost" of the "♭," as it was smoothed out imperfectly from the copper engraving plate.

c) In the first edition  B and D are engraver's errors.

INTRODUZIONE
Adagio molto (♪ = 50)

d) Thus in the first edition, perhaps through a misunderstanding; the better solution is since it is more important to emphasize the dissonance between C and D. In addition, the C continues a progression in the bass; the second B-flat does not.

RONDO
Allegretto moderato (♩ = 104)

Attacca subito il Rondo:

e) Beethoven's pedal markings create a delicate, diaphanous sonic mist. Contrary to common expectation, these pedal markings are challenging on both contemporaneous fortepianos and on modern instruments. However, the challenges are different. The pedal/damper technology on fortepianos is less precise than that of our modern grands, which in turn have greater sonorous capability. f) The motive starts with the low G. g) Some editions erroneously print a g3 instead of f 3.

h) First sixteenth note is detached to designate the beginning of the motive. i) Continue seamlessly the trill already in motion.

j) The last eighth rest denotes the release of the damper pedal.

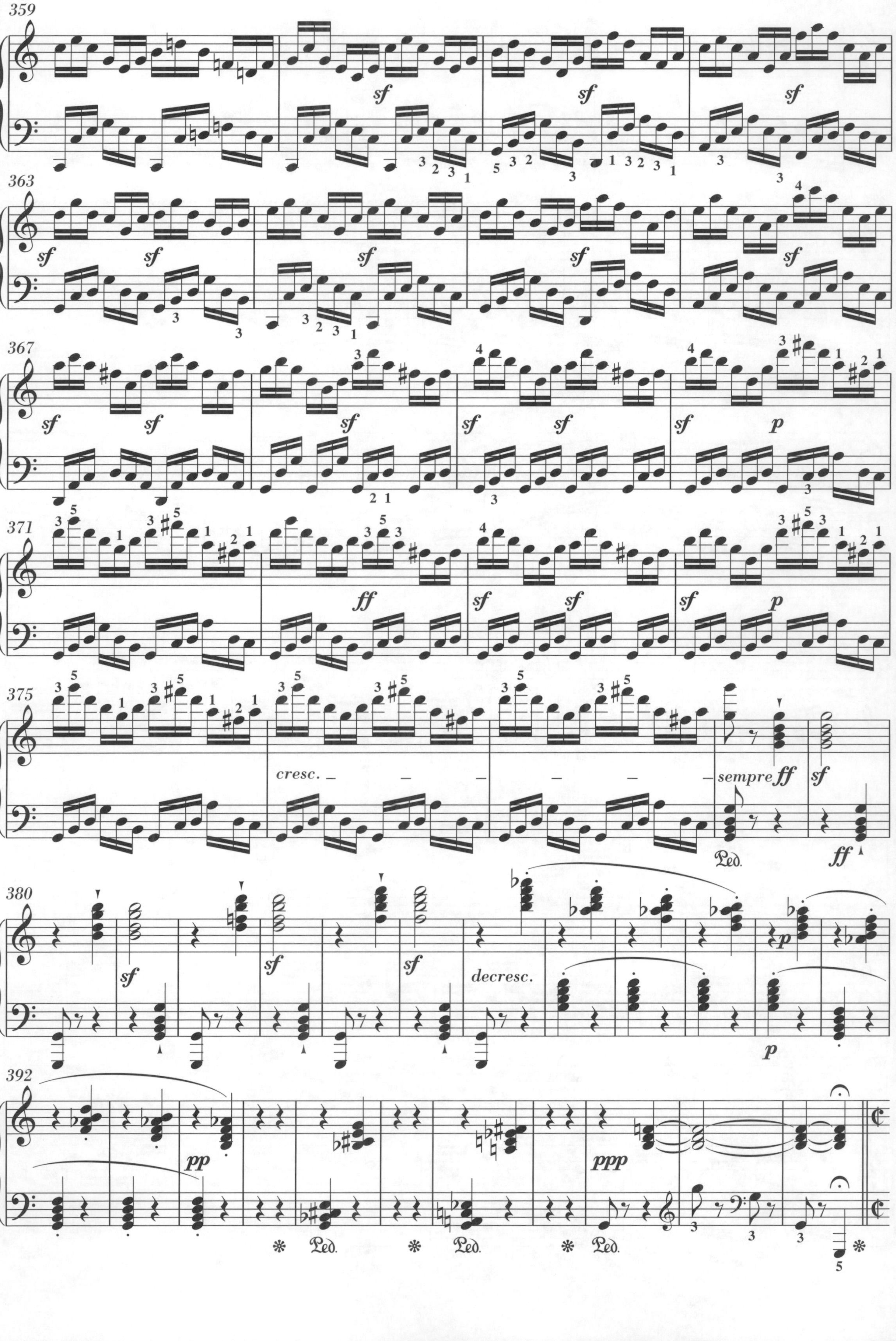
359
363
367
371
375
cresc.
sempre ff
380
decresc.
392
pp
ppp
Ped.

k) Beethoven's fingering, coupled with the fact that he provided no suggested simplification of this passage (as he did in the trills beginning in m. 485), implies that one hand plays an octave glissando; perfectly possible in—and consistent with—the context of this whirlwind Prestissimo Coda.

1) In the autograph manuscript, Beethoven noted: "Those for whom the trill, in combination with the theme, is too difficult, may simplify it the following way:

or if they are able to, may double it:

Two notes of each sextuplet are played to each quarter note in the bass. It doesn't matter if this trill loses some of its normal speed."

Sonata in F Major

Opus 54
Composed in 1804

In tempo d'un Menuetto (♩ = 100)

22.

a) In the first edition, the A-flat–B-flat–C octaves begin here (second beat), in contrast to the analogous phrase in m. 33.

b) short appoggiatura

126

c) The editor suggests ⊔⊔ ⊔⊔

d) without tail

128

e) The E, E-flat, and D are in parentheses because Beethoven's pianos at this time did not extend lower than F.

f) The first edition has D-natural here, rather than D-flat. g) The first edition has A here, rather than B-double flat.

h) LH over RH

Dedicated to Prince Franz von Brunswick

Sonata in F minor

Opus 57
Composed in 1804–05

a) Pedal markings are Beethoven's. b) Start ornament with C on the beat.

136

c) 𝄞 etc. d) In autograph and first edition, E instead of F-flat, but both have F-flat in m. 57.

e) No afterbeat to this trill in both the autograph and the first edition.

f) These cadenza-like flourishes (mm. 227–235) follow the distribution of hands as per the autograph and first edition; any other distribution would lessen the expressive and schematic impact of this passage.

g) LH under RH

Andante con moto ($\flat$ = 92)

154

h) The tie is expressly present in the autograph, although it is not included in some editions.

i) 4 is suggested when leading into second ending.

Dedicated to Countess Therese von Brunswick

Sonata in F-sharp Major

Opus 78
Composed in 1809

Adagio cantabile (♪ = 63) **Allegro ma non troppo** (♩ = 63)

24.

a) The fingering in italics and the pedal markings are Beethoven's. b) In the autograph and first edition (Breitkopf & Härtel), the *sf* appears as placed (first beat of m. 17) in this edition. Several other editions place this *sf* on the fourth beat of m. 16 in order to be consistent with its placement in the recapitulation (m. 75), also as per the autograph and first edition. (See footnote for m. 75) c) d) Several other editions print the chords in this measure as in order to be consistent with the F-double sharp in the right hand.

e) See footnote for m. 16. The placement of the *sf* in m. 75 is consistent with the autograph score and first edition. f) See footnote for m. 25. The C-natural in the LH is consistent with the autograph score and first edition. g) *ff* here (compared to *f* in m. 26) as per the autograph.

h) Addition of an F-sharp on the fourth beat—as per several other editions, perhaps an attempt at consistency with the second beat—is wrong. The autograph
score is clearly notated with the F-sharp–G–E (beats 2, 3, 4) as a separate voice.

170

i) LH over RH

j) The suspension of strict meter in this measure—which is written very broadly by Beethoven in his autograph score—continues and heightens the cadential suspense begun in the previous two measures.

Sonata in G Major

Opus 79
Composed in 1809

Presto alla tedesca (♩. = 80)

a) The pedal markings are Beethoven's. b) Note the differences in harmonies in mm. 5, 56, and 127.

c) without tail d) See footnote to m. 5. e) Still generally *f* here, in contrast to *p* in mm. 66–74. Measures 83–89 and mm. 90–98 offer the same dynamic contrast.

f) See footnote to m. 5. g) The three notes B–A–G-sharp fit within the last part of the second beat. h) without tail

i) A few editions, including the first edition, have a G here instead of the B-flat. The interval of the sixth here seems more consistent with the character of this movement thus far, reserving octaves for m. 30 onwards.

j) Short appoggiatura (less than a sixteenth in value).

Upon the Departure of Archduke Rudolph, Vienna, 4th May 1809

Sonata in E-flat Major

Opus 81a
Composed in 1809

attacca subito l'Allegro

a) Despite Beethoven's expressly stated title "Das Lebewohl," the first edition is entitled "Sonate caractéristique: Les adieux, l'absence, et le retour." This misrepresentation was often criticized by Beethoven. b) The fingering in italics and the pedal markings are Beethoven's.

184

c) In the autograph score, a *p* in this measure replaces an erased ⟩ ; hence the parentheses around the *p* in m. 94.

186

d) The legato slur here is in accordance with the autograph manuscript and first edition, and contrasts with the slurs in mm. 23–24. e) The LH passage is in accordance with the autograph manuscript and first edition, and contrasts with the parallel passage in m. 25.

f) The autograph includes a D in this chord; early editions do not.

ABWESENHEIT
Andante espressivo (♪ = 69)
In gehender Bewegung, doch mit Ausdruck

g) The low E was not present in Beethoven's fortepiano at this time. Only with Sonata Op. 101 did Beethoven first use this note in a piano work, since fortepianos of 1816 included it.

192

WIEDERSEHEN
Vivacissimamente (♩. = 112)
Im lebhaftesten Zeitmaasse

Im Januar 1810

h) without tail

Dedicated to Prince Moritz von Lichnowsky

Sonata in E minor

Opus 90
Composed in 1814

Mit Lebhaftigkeit und durchaus mit Empfindung und Ausdruck (♩ = 138)

27.

a) LH under RH

b) LH under RH

c) In the first edition, no octave on the first eighth; hence the fingering suggested.

d) This low E was not present in Beethoven's fortepiano at this time. Only with Sonata Op. 101 did Beethoven first include this note in a score, since pianos of 1816 included it.

Nicht zu geschwind und sehr singbar vorzutragen (♩ = 80)

e) In the first edition, F-sharp is a quarter note, not an eighth note as it is in subsequent printings.

f) Some editions erroneously notate the B in the bass as a quarter note.   g) Some editions erroneously notate the lowest note of this chord as D-sharp rather than F-sharp.

Dedicated to Baroness Dorothea Ertmann

Sonata in A Major

Opus 101
Composed in 1816

Etwas lebhaft und mit der innigsten Empfindung (♩. = 63)
Allegretto, ma non troppo

28.

a) The fingering in italics is Beethoven's.

219

b) Thus in Beethoven's autograph score. The first edition deletes the G-sharp on the second eighth and ties the E from the second to the third eighth. We assume the autograph to be correct.

Lebhaft. [c)] **Marschmäßig** (♩ = 152)

Vivace alla Marcia

d) Thus in the autograph score. In the first edition, the C (LH, first beat) in mm. 52 and 53 are both notated as quarter notes.  Since it cannot be determined whether or not this latter notation is a correction by Beethoven, we recommend the version printed (autograph).

224

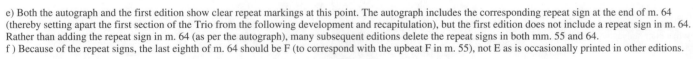

e) Both the autograph and the first edition show clear repeat markings at this point. The autograph includes the corresponding repeat sign at the end of m. 64 (thereby setting apart the first section of the Trio from the following development and recapitulation), but the first edition does not include a repeat sign in m. 64. Rather than adding the repeat sign in m. 64 (as per the autograph), many subsequent editions delete the repeat signs in both mm. 55 and 64.

f) Because of the repeat signs, the last eighth of m. 64 should be F (to correspond with the upbeat F in m. 55), not E as is occasionally printed in other editions.

Marcia dal segno al Fine senza repetizione

226

Langsam und sehnsuchtsvoll (♪ = 46)
Adagio, ma non troppo, con affetto

Sul una corda
Mit einer Saite

Nach und nach mehrere Saiten
poco a poco tutte le corde

non presto

Zeitmaß des ersten Stückes
Tempo del primo pezzo: tutto il cembalo ma piano

Geschwind, doch nicht zu sehr, und mit Entschlossenheit (♩ = 120)

230

g) This tie appears in the autograph score, but not in the first edition.

Dedicated to Archduke Rudolph

Sonata in B-flat Major
(Sonate für das Hammerklavier)

Opus 106
Composed 1817–1818

a) The metronome markings, pedal markings, and fingering in italics are Beethoven's.

238

b) RH over LH c) RH over LH

d) RH over LH e) The autograph of Op. 106 remains lost. The placement of slurs in the first edition is unclear here; both the RH and LH slurs may extend across the barline, linking mm. 61–62 with m. 63. f) No middle voice in the first edition. The C–E is occasionally suggested as a possible voice "for consistency," but the sound is more brilliant without them.

g) This notation, assuming it faithfully depicts the autograph, represents aspects of Beethoven's manner of playing. h) These slurs (mm. 149, 151, 164, 168–172) are not in the first edition. I have followed later editions here.

i) The Artaria edition does not include these sharps before these Gs in m. 210 and m. 212; however, the first English edition does. See Performance Notes.

j) I believe A-sharp to be correct here. See Performance Notes.

k) D-flat instead of D in the first edition.

249

SCHERZO
Assai vivace ♩. = 80

1) This B-flat is not present in the first edition.

Adagio sostenuto ♪ = **92**
Appassionato e con molto sentimento

m) As per the first edition. Several later editions have an A-sharp here.

n) As per first edition; some later editions leave out the A in the bass.

o) Not present on Beethoven's piano. I play only the top C-sharp here.

264

p) As per the first edition. Later editions print a G here as an appoggiatura. q) In the first edition there are no ties here. r) See Performance Notes.

266

Per la misura si conta nel largo sempre quattro semicrome, cio è ♪ ♪ ♪ ♪

s) As per the first edition. Later editions print ɣ···.

t) The trill is of primary motivic importance, but the Nachschlag (tail) is not. Consequently these are instances in which Beethoven did not include the Nachschlag.

u) In the first edition there are no accidentals in front of the E-flats in mm. 33 and 35. Subsequent editions have natural signs. I believe E-flat is correct.

v) No flat in the first edition. G-flat is consistent with the intervallic complexion of the theme.

w) The tie is not present in the first edition.

274

x) The tie linking the Ds is not present in the first edition.

276

y) RH

278

z) The natural signs in front of the Cs are not present in the first edition, but some subsequent editions print them. I believe that C-sharps are correct here.

sempre ben marcato

284

Dedicated to Maximiliane Brentano
Sonata in E Major

Opus 109
Composed in 1820

a) As per the autograph. The first edition is Vivace ma non troppo.

b) The autograph contains a bar line at this point (between the G-sharp and A-sharp).

c) The *p* initially at this point in the autograph is crossed out in pencil, with the *f* (also in pencil) added under the chord.

d) The pedal marking in the autograph clearly links these two movements. There is no silence or interruption between them. In addition, the "issimo" of "Prestissimo" was added by Beethoven in the autograph in pencil; see discussion.

e) without tail

f) without tail

Gesangvoll, mit innigster Empfindung (♩ = 60)
Andante molto cantabile ed espressivo

g) Based on examination of Beethoven's autograph score, I suggest no explicit *ritardando* in this measure (and subsequent last measures of variations as well), thus resulting in a seamless, uninterrupted musical journey through the entire movement. The only true *ritardando* is in the final measure in the recurrence of the theme. See Performance Notes.

VAR. II
leggiermente

VAR. III
allegro vivace

VAR. IV
etwas langsamer, als das Thema
un poco meno andante ciò è un poco più adagio come il tema

g) In the autograph the fourth eighth note is clearly D-sharp, although the first edition has a B here.

h) **allegro ma non troppo**

h) Beethoven abandons "variation" designation at this point, for the formal structure here is longer than the theme and previous variations; see Performance Notes.
"Var. V" is stated in the first edition.

tempo primo del tema ⁱ⁾

i) "Var. VI" in the first edition, but not in the autograph.

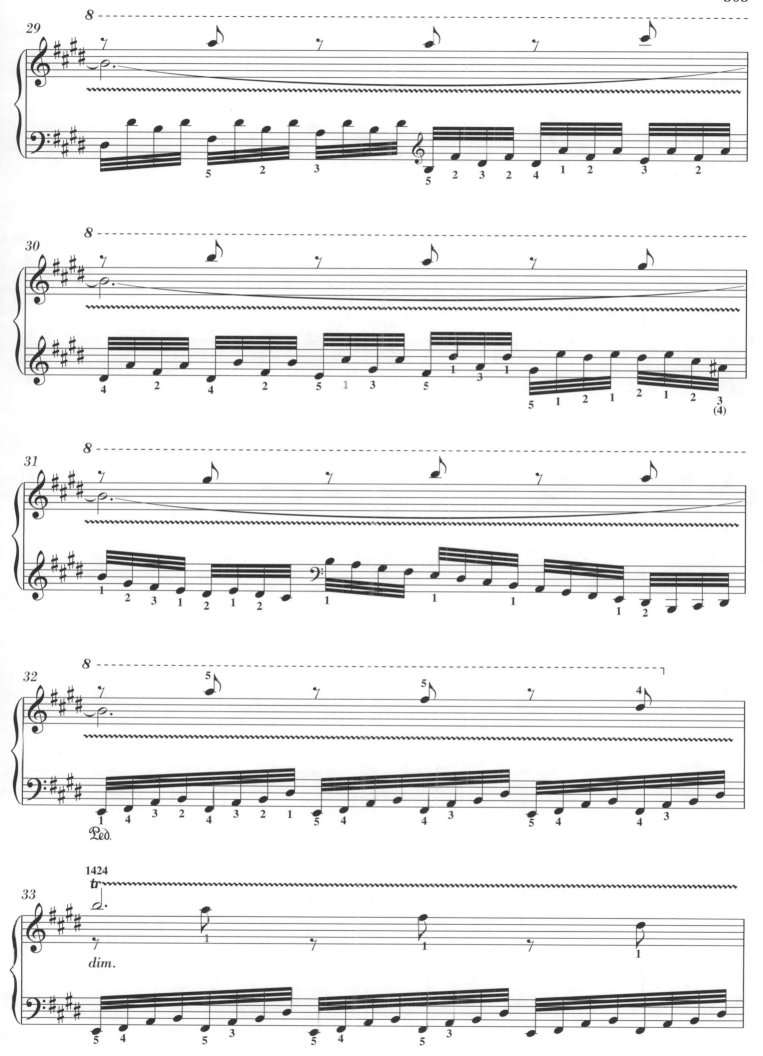

Sonata in A-flat Major

Opus 110
Composed in 1821

Moderato cantabile molto espressivo (♩. = 63)

31.

a) The fingering in italics and the pedal markings are Beethoven's.

309

b) In the autograph, this LH slur extends across the bar line (which is at the end of a system), implying extra weightiness. c) This LH slur is present in the autograph, but not in a fair copy (in an unknown hand) owned by Brahms.

FUGA

Allegra ma non troppo (♩. = 80-84)

L'istesso tempo di Arioso

(Ermattet klagend)
Perdendo le forze, dolente

320 **L'istesso tempo della Fuga**
poi a poi di nuovo vivente
Nach und nach wieder auflebend

sempre una corda
L'inversione della Fuga (Die Umkehrung der Fuge)

poi a poi tutte le corde

Meno allegro. Etwas langsamer

d) *m.d.*

d) As per the autograph score

e) As per autograph f) The autograph includes "Tempo primo" on the fourth beat of m. 174, the point at which the Fugue theme returns triumphantly in bass octaves, forte. The acceleration begun with the double diminution in m. 168 culminates at this point. The "Tempo Primo" is not present in the fair copy (unknown hand) in Brahms' possession, nor is it in the first edition. However, there is no evidence that Beethoven deleted—or wished to delete—this marking.

g) E-flat in the autograph, but D-flat in the first edition and the fair copy (unknown hand) owned by Brahms.

Dedicated to Archduke Rudolph

Sonata in C minor

Opus 111
Composed in 1822

a) The fingering in italics and the pedal markings are Beethoven's.

b) Many editions suggest *sf* markings for the D-flat and D-natural (mm. 48–49) even though there are none in the autograph. I have chosen not to suggest them here, for this chromatic D-flat–D-natural progression is functionally different from the falling fifth C–F (mm. 114–115). The latter includes an *sf* marking, and presages the descending fifth of the coda (m. 150).

c) Some editions make the C a C-flat, although there is no ♭ sign in the autograph. I believe C is correct.

d) Pedal as per autograph. e) There is no $>$ $\boldsymbol{p}$ (as is often printed here) in the autograph. One may naturally shape the dynamics down (softer) here, but the establishment of a stable C Major is a reason to not be diminuative. f) The first edition is G–E-natural–G, not G–C–E-natural as written in the autograph.

g) Not present in the autograph. One could sustain the pedal until the first chord of the Arietta.

ARIETTA
Adagio molto semplice e cantabile ($\flat$ = 100)

h) This tie is not present in the autograph, but does appear in the first edition.

i) These ties are not present in both the autograph and the first edition.

j) The E here is correct, as per both the autograph and the first edition.

k) As per the autograph.

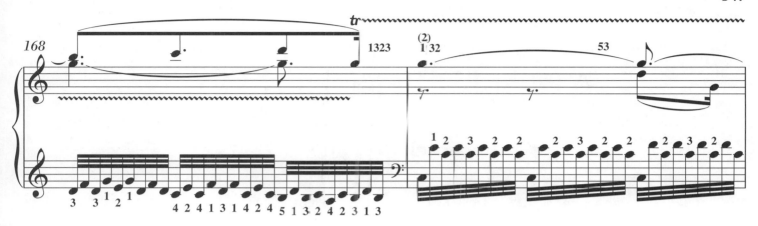

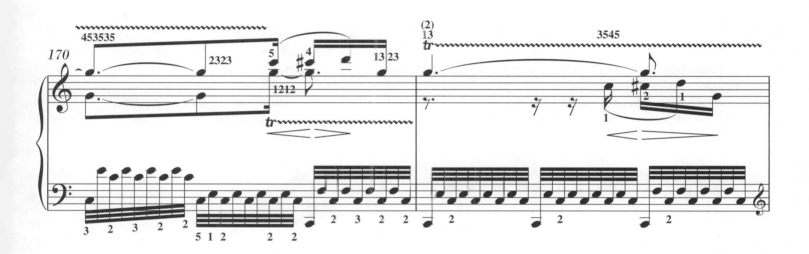

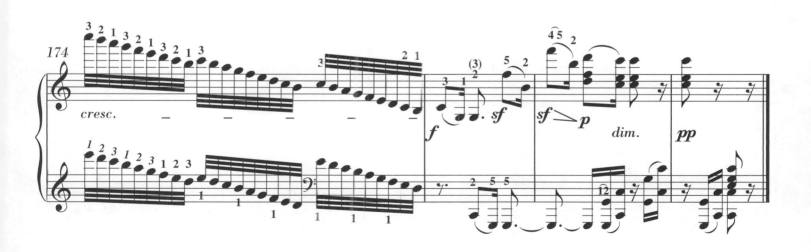

ABOUT THE EDITOR

ROBERT TAUB

From New York's Carnegie Hall to Hong Kong's Cultural Centre to Germany's *avant garde* Zentrum für Kunst und Medientechnologie, Robert Taub is acclaimed internationally. He has performed as soloist with the MET Orchestra in Carnegie Hall, the Boston Symphony Orchestra, BBC Philharmonic, The Philadelphia Orchestra, San Francisco Symphony, Los Angeles Philharmonic, Montreal Symphony, Munich Philharmonic, Orchestra of St. Luke's, Hong Kong Philharmonic, Singapore Symphony, and others.

Robert Taub has performed solo recitals on the Great Performers Series at New York's Lincoln Center and other major series worldwide. He has been featured in international festivals, including the Saratoga Festival, the Lichfield Festival in England, San Francisco's Midsummer Mozart Festival, the Geneva International Summer Festival, among others.

Following the conclusion of his highly celebrated New York series of Beethoven Piano Sonatas, Taub completed a sold-out Beethoven cycle in London at Hampton Court Palace. His recordings of the complete Beethoven Piano Sonatas have been praised throughout the world for their insight, freshness, and emotional involvement. In addition to performing, Robert Taub is an eloquent spokesman for music, giving frequent engaging and informal lectures and pre-concert talks. His book on Beethoven—*Playing the Beethoven Piano Sonatas*—has been published internationally by Amadeus Press.

Taub was featured in a recent PBS television program—*Big Ideas*—that highlighted him playing and discussing Beethoven Piano Sonatas. Filmed during his time as Artist-in-Residence at the Institute for Advanced Study, this program has been broadcast throughout the US on PBS affiliates.

Robert Taub's performances are frequently broadcast on radio networks around the world, including the NPR (Performance Today), Ireland's RTE, and Hong Kong's RTHK. He has also recorded the Sonatas of Scriabin and works of Beethoven, Schumann, Liszt, and Babbitt for Harmonia Mundi, several of which have been selected as "critic's favorites" by *Gramophone*, *Newsweek*, *The New York Times*, *The Washington Post*, *Ovation*, and *Fanfare*.

Robert Taub is involved with contemporary music as well as the established literature, premiering piano concertos by Milton Babbitt (MET Orchestra, James Levine) and Mel Powell (Los Angeles Philharmonic), and making the first recordings of the Persichetti Piano Concerto (Philadelphia Orchestra, Charles Dutoit) and Sessions Piano Concerto. He has premiered six works of Milton Babbitt (solo piano, chamber music, Second Piano Concerto). Taub has also collaborated with several 21st-century composers, including Jonathan Dawe (USA), David Bessell (UK), and Ludger Brümmer (Germany) performing their works in America and Europe.

Taub is a Phi Beta Kappa graduate of Princeton where he was a University Scholar. As a Danforth Fellow he completed his doctoral degree at The Juilliard School where he received the highest award in piano. Taub has served as Artist-in-Residence at Harvard University, at UC Davis, as well as at the Institute for Advanced Study. He has led music forums at Oxford and Cambridge Universities and The Juilliard School. Taub has also been Visiting Professor at Princeton University and at Kingston University (UK).